Butterfly Tissue Box

Size: Fits boutique-style tissue box
Skill Level: Beginner

Materials

- ❑ 2 sheets clear 7-count plastic canvas
- ❑ Medium weight yarn as listed in color key
- ❑ #16 tapestry needle

Stitching Step by Step

1 Cut top and one each of sides A, B, C and D from plastic canvas according to graphs.

2 Stitch plastic canvas according to graphs, filling in uncoded areas with white Continental Stitches.

3 Using black yarn throughout, Straight Stitch antennae on butterflies on top and sides, and tails on butterflies on top. Work French Knots at ends of antennae on sides, wrapping yarn once around needle for each knot.

4 Using white yarn throughout, Overcast opening in tissue cover top. Whipstitch sides to one another along corners; Overcast bottom edges. Whipstitch assembled sides to top.

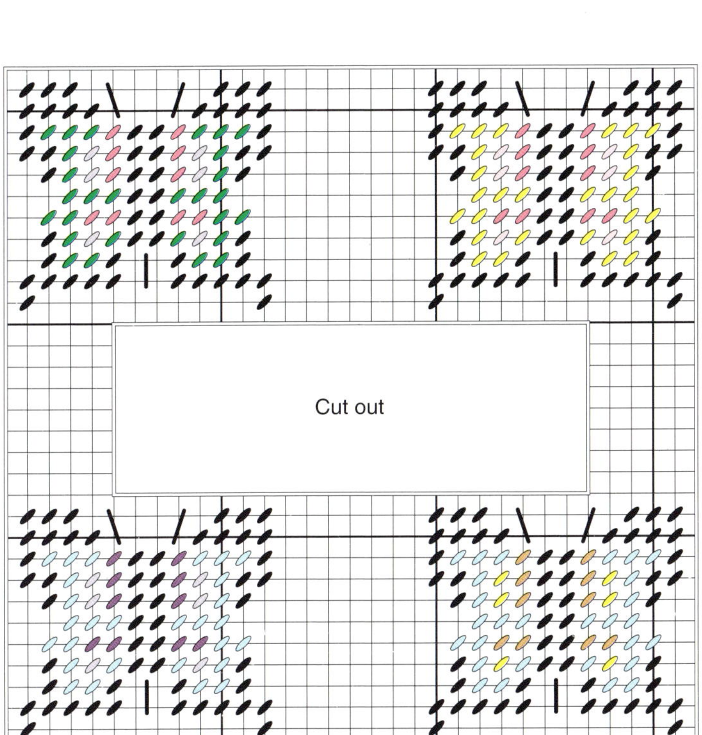

Butterfly Tissue Box Top
32 holes x 32 holes
Cut 1

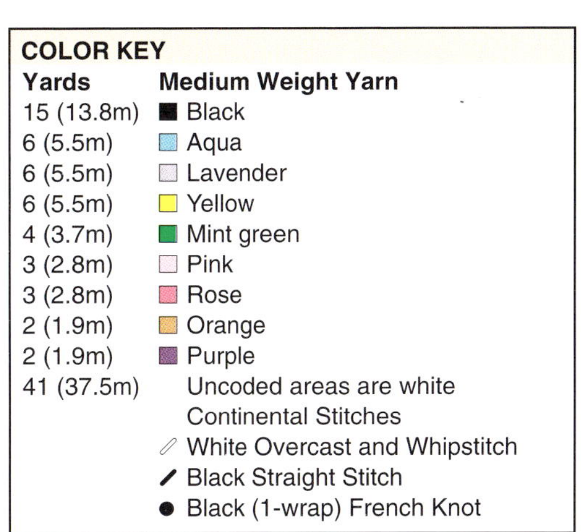

COLOR KEY

Yards	Medium Weight Yarn
15 (13.8m)	■ Black
6 (5.5m)	■ Aqua
6 (5.5m)	■ Lavender
6 (5.5m)	■ Yellow
4 (3.7m)	■ Mint green
3 (2.8m)	■ Pink
3 (2.8m)	■ Rose
2 (1.9m)	■ Orange
2 (1.9m)	■ Purple
41 (37.5m)	Uncoded areas are white Continental Stitches
	⁄ White Overcast and Whipstitch
	⁄ Black Straight Stitch
	● Black (1-wrap) French Knot

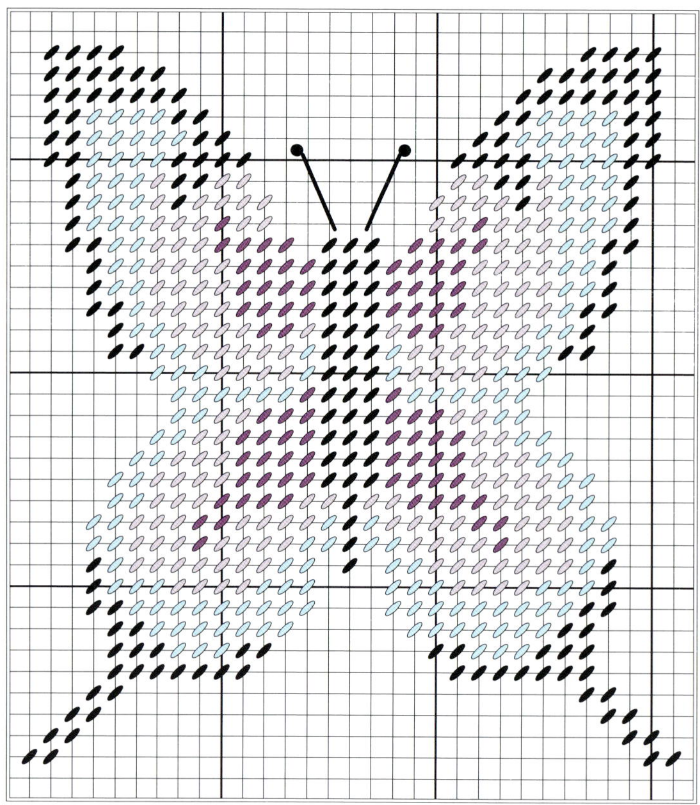

Butterfly Tissue Box Side A
32 holes x 37 holes
Cut 1

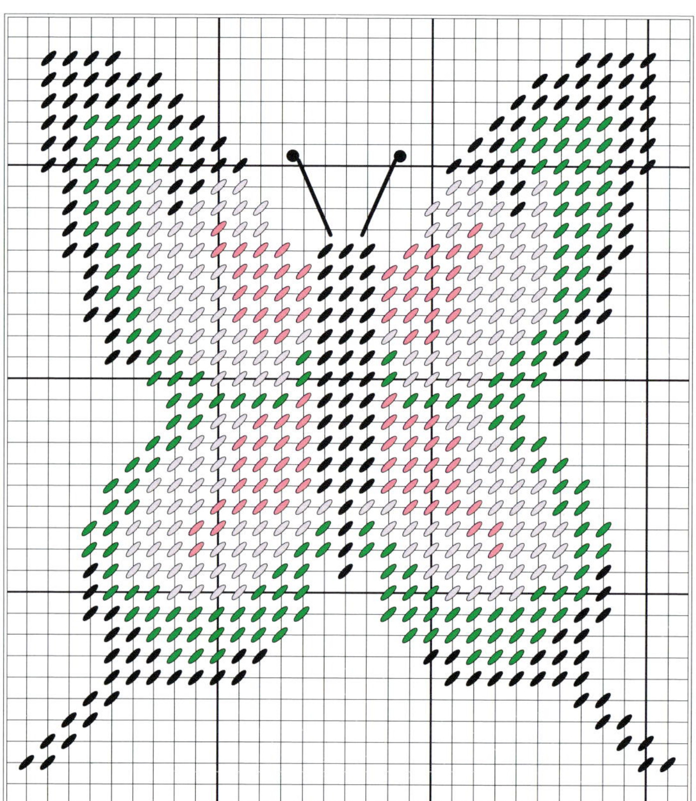

Butterfly Tissue Box Side B
32 holes x 37 holes
Cut 1

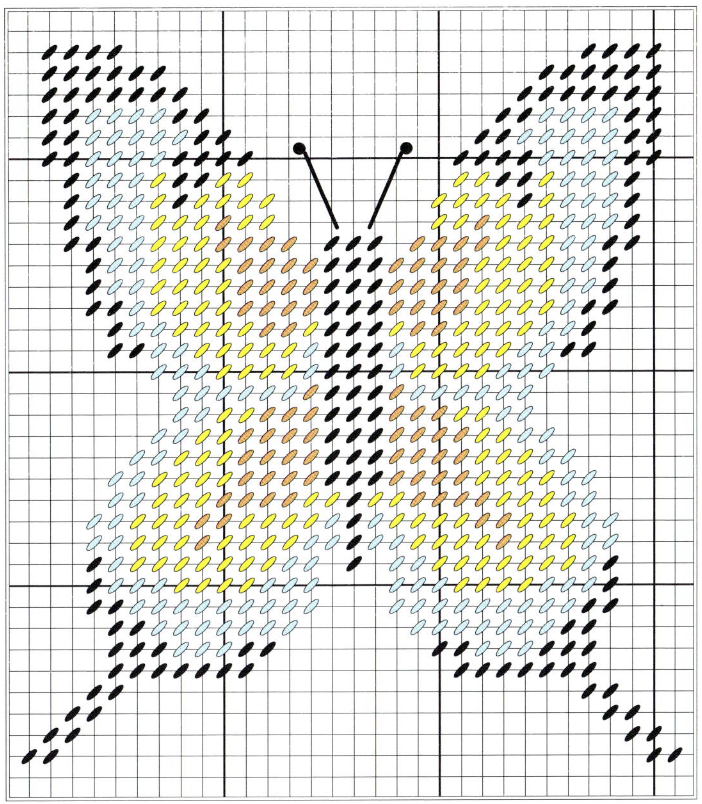

Butterfly Tissue Box Side C
32 holes x 37 holes
Cut 1

COLOR KEY	
Yards	**Medium Weight Yarn**
15 (13.8m)	■ Black
6 (5.5m)	■ Aqua
6 (5.5m)	■ Lavender
6 (5.5m)	■ Yellow
4 (3.7m)	■ Mint green
3 (2.8m)	■ Pink
3 (2.8m)	■ Rose
2 (1.9m)	■ Orange
2 (1.9m)	■ Purple
41 (37.5m)	Uncoded areas are white Continental Stitches
	White Overcast and Whipstitch
	Black Straight Stitch
	● Black (1-wrap) French Knot

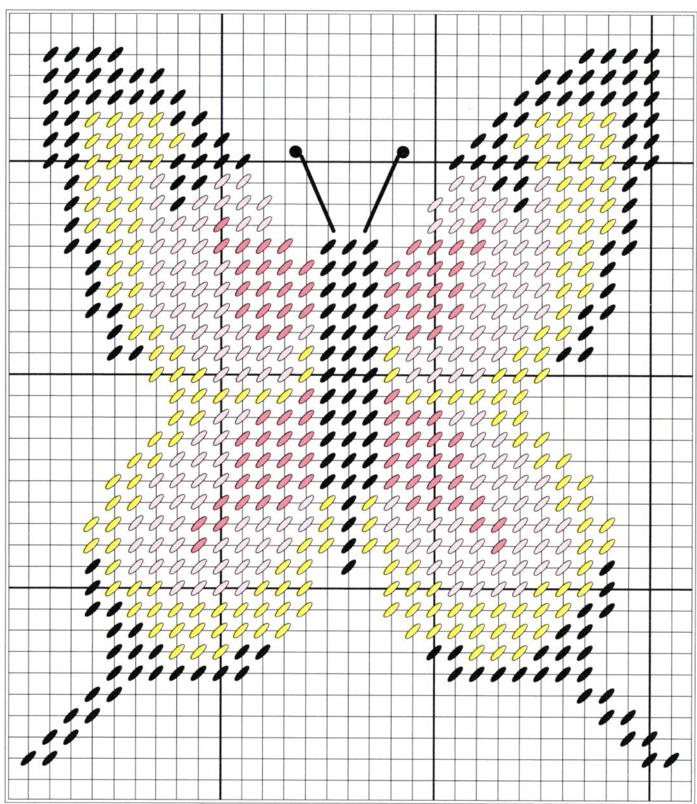

Butterfly Tissue Box Side D
32 holes x 37 holes
Cut 1

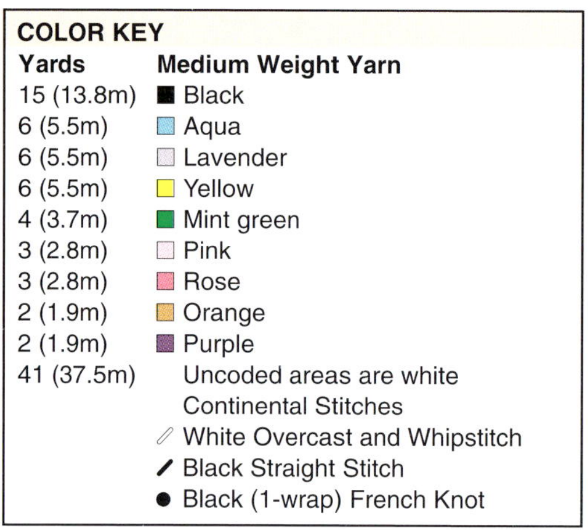

COLOR KEY

Yards	Medium Weight Yarn
15 (13.8m)	■ Black
6 (5.5m)	■ Aqua
6 (5.5m)	■ Lavender
6 (5.5m)	■ Yellow
4 (3.7m)	■ Mint green
3 (2.8m)	■ Pink
3 (2.8m)	■ Rose
2 (1.9m)	■ Orange
2 (1.9m)	■ Purple
41 (37.5m)	Uncoded areas are white Continental Stitches
	⁄ White Overcast and Whipstitch
	⁄ Black Straight Stitch
	● Black (1-wrap) French Knot

Bag Holder

Size: 4½ inches W x 18 inches H x 2½ inches D (11.4cm x 45.7m x 6.4cm), excluding butterflies
Skill Level: Beginner

Materials

- ❑ 3 sheets clear 7-count plastic canvas
- ❑ Medium weight yarn as listed in color key
- ❑ #16 tapestry needle

Stitching Step by Step

Butterflies

1 Cut two pairs of butterfly wings from plastic canvas according to graphs.

2 Stitch one pair of wings according to graphs. Stitch the second pair substituting blue for light purple and dark blue for purple.

3 Using black yarn, Whipstitch matching pairs of wings together between arrows; Overcast remaining edges.

4 Work yellow Straight Stitches on both butterflies.

5 *Antennae:* Cut two 4-inch (10cm) pieces of black yarn; fold each in half. Referring to photo throughout, hot-glue folded end of antennae to reverse side of each butterfly.

Bag Holder

1 Cut bag holder front, back, tab and bottom from plastic canvas according to graphs, joining graphs for front's top and bottom portions before cutting front in one piece.

2 Stitch front and tab according to graphs. Back and bottom will remain unstitched.

3 Straight Stitch flower centers using yellow yarn.

4 Using black yarn and referring to photo, tack centers of butterflies to front where indicated by red lines on front graphs.

5 Using off-white yarn throughout, Overcast tab's side and bottom edges; Whipstitch top edge to bag holder back where indicated by red line on graph.

6 Whipstitch side edges of stitched front to matching edges of back, positioning tab on back *inside* bag holder. Overcast top edges.

7 Position bag holder bottom in opening at bottom. Whipstitch adjacent edges to front and back. Overcast remaining edges of front only; diagonal edges of bottom remain unfinished.

8 Insert plastic bags into holder through top; pull bags out through opening at bottom.

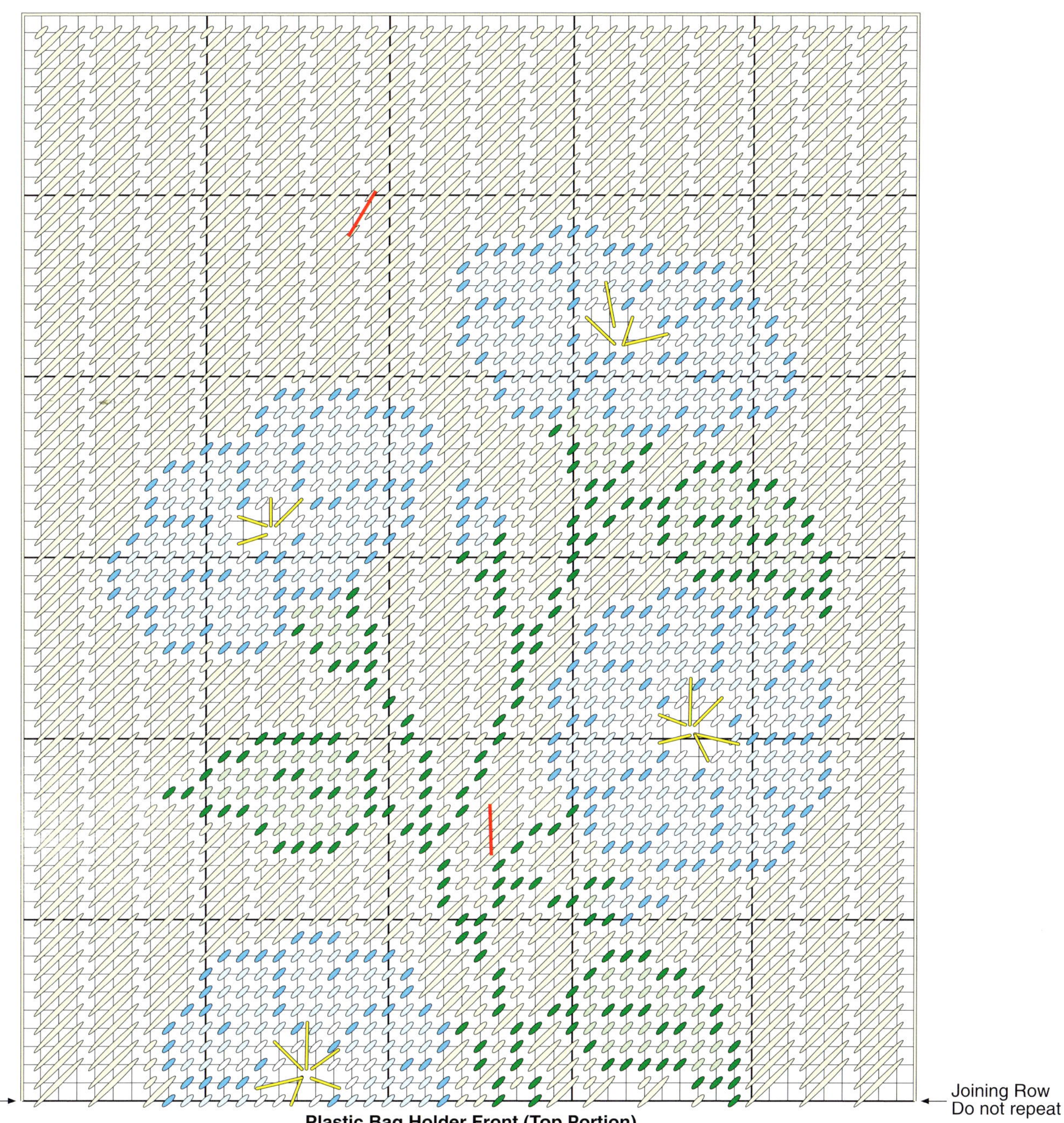

Plastic Bag Holder Front (Top Portion)
49 holes x 120 holes
Cut 1
Join with graph for bottom portion
before cutting as 1 piece

COLOR KEY

Yards	Medium Weight Yarn
44 (40.3m)	Off-white
10 (9.2m)	Light blue
9 (8.3m)	Blue
5 (4.6m)	Black
3 (2.8m)	Dark green
3 (2.8m)	Green
2 (1.9m)	Dark blue
2 (1.9m)	Light purple
2 (1.9m)	Purple
2 (1.9m)	White
2 (1.9m)	Yellow Straight Stitch

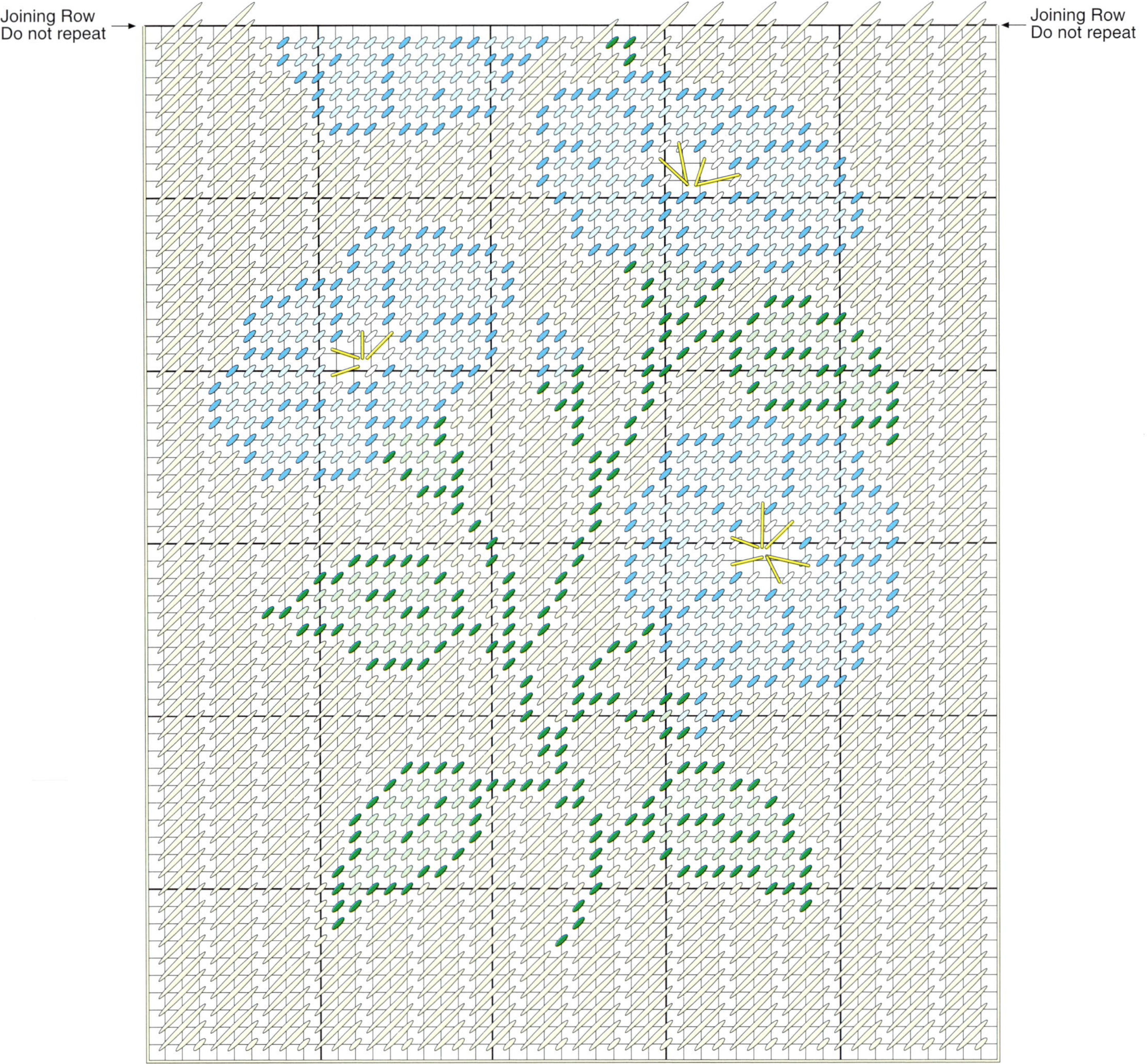

Plastic Bag Holder Front (Bottom Portion)
49 holes x 120 holes
Cut 1
Join with graph for top portion
before cutting as 1 piece

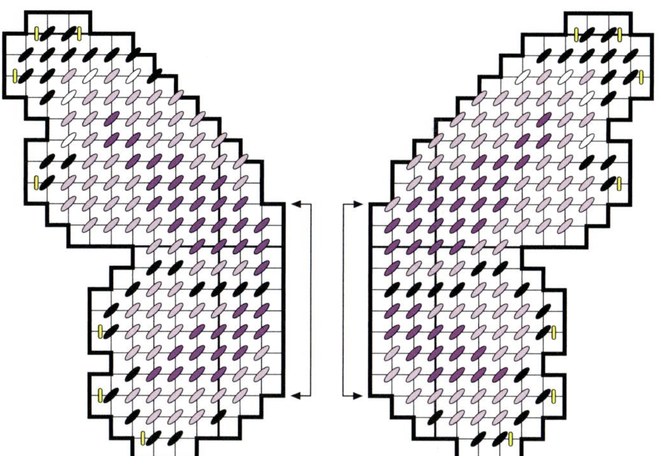

Plastic Bag Holder Butterfly Wings
13 holes x 21 holes
Cut 2 pairs
Stitch 1 pair as shown; stitch 1 pair substituting blue for light purple and dark blue for purple

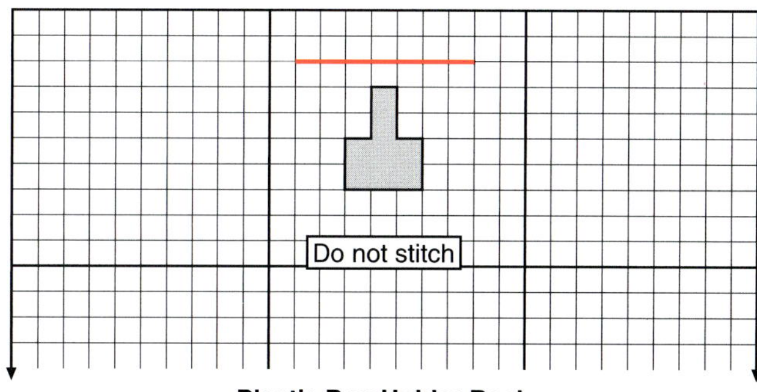

Plastic Bag Holder Back
29 holes x 120 holes
Cut 1, cutting away gray area; do not stitch

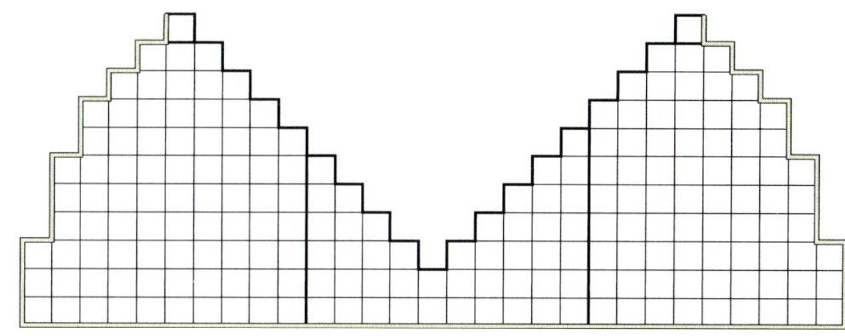

Plastic Bag Holder Bottom
29 holes x 11 holes
Cut 1, do not stitch

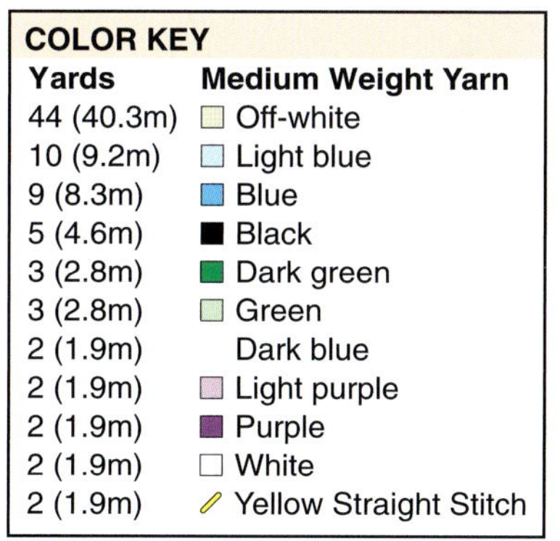

COLOR KEY

Yards	Medium Weight Yarn
44 (40.3m)	Off-white
10 (9.2m)	Light blue
9 (8.3m)	Blue
5 (4.6m)	Black
3 (2.8m)	Dark green
3 (2.8m)	Green
2 (1.9m)	Dark blue
2 (1.9m)	Light purple
2 (1.9m)	Purple
2 (1.9m)	White
2 (1.9m)	Yellow Straight Stitch

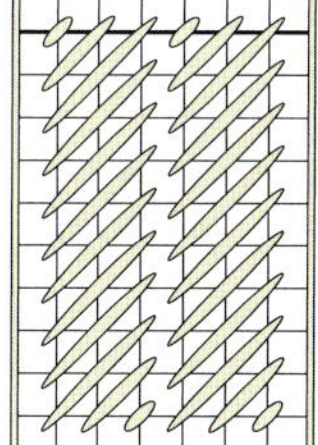

Plastic Bag Holder Tab
7 holes x 11 holes
Cut 1

Coasters

Size: **Coasters:** 4⅝ inches W x 4¾ inches H (11.4cm x 12.1cm)
Holder: 4⅜ inches W x 1⅞ inches H x 1¾ inches D (11.1cm x 4.8cm x 4.4cm)
Skill Level: Beginner

Materials

- ❑ 2 sheets clear 7-count plastic canvas
- ❑ Medium weight yarn as listed in color key
- ❑ 2 black chenille stems
- ❑ #16 tapestry needle
- ❑ Wire cutters *or* craft nippers
- ❑ Hot-glue gun

Stitching Step by Step

1 Cut coaster holder front and back and two each of butterflies A, C and D, pages 20 and 21, from plastic canvas according to graphs. Also cut two pieces 11 holes x 12 holes for coaster holder sides and one piece 28 holes x 11 holes for coaster holder bottom; bottom will remain unstitched.

2 Stitch butterflies A, C and D according to graphs, filling in uncoded areas with black Continental Stitches. Overcast butterflies with adjacent colors according to graphs.

3 *Antennae:* Using wire cutters, cut six 4-inch (10cm) pieces from chenille stems. Bend each into a V; curl ends toward outside. Referring to photo throughout, hot-glue base of antennae to reverse side of each butterfly.

4 Stitch coaster holder front and back according to graphs, filling in uncoded areas with white Continental Stitches; fill in coaster holder sides with white Continental Stitches

5 Using black yarn, Straight Stitch antennae and tails on butterflies on coaster holder front and back.

6 Using white yarn throughout, Whipstitch front, back and sides to one another along corners; Overcast top edges. Whipstitch assembled front, back and sides to bottom. Tuck coasters into holder.

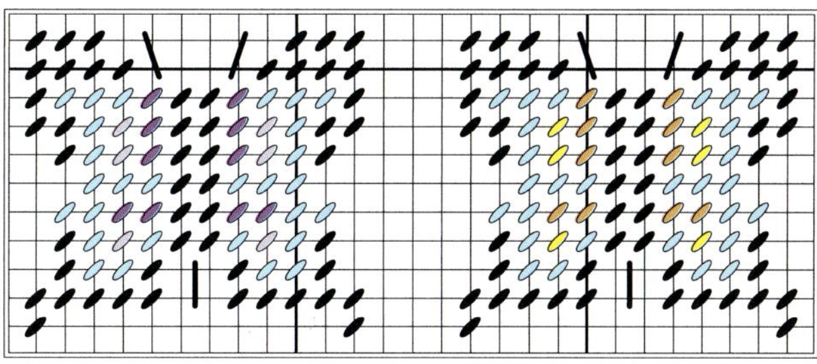

Coaster Holder Front
28 holes x 12 holes
Cut 1

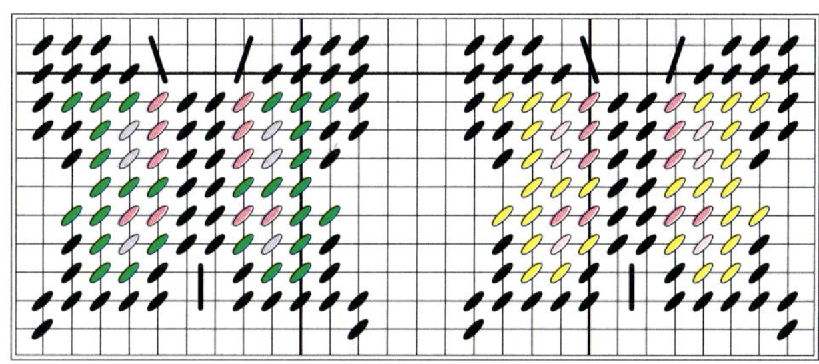

Coaster Holder Back
28 holes x 12 holes
Cut 1

COLOR KEY	
Yards	**Medium Weight Yarn**
27 (24.7m)	■ Black
14 (12.9m)	□ Aqua
6 (5.5m)	□ Yellow
5 (4.6m)	□ Lavender
5 (4.6m)	□ Pink
3 (2.8m)	□ Orange
3 (2.8m)	□ Rose
3 (2.8m)	□ Purple
1 (1m)	■ Mint green
41 (37.5m)	Uncoded areas on coaster holder front and back are white Continental Stitches
	White Overcast and Whipstitch
	Uncoded areas on butterflies A, C and D are black Continental Stitches
	/ Black Straight Stitch

Magnets

Size: 2⅝ inches W x 2⅛ inches H (6.7cm x 5.4cm) excluding antennae
Skill Level: Beginner

Materials

Set of 3 Magnets

- ❑ 1 sheet clear 7-count plastic canvas
- ❑ Medium weight yarn as listed in color key
- ❑ Black chenille stem
- ❑ #16 tapestry needle
- ❑ 3 (1-inch/2.5cm) pieces magnetic tape *or* button magnets
- ❑ Wire cutters *or* craft nippers
- ❑ Hot-glue gun

Project Note

Materials and yarn amounts are for a set of three magnets, one in each color scheme.

Stitching Step by Step

1 Cut one pair of butterfly wings for each magnet from plastic canvas according to graphs.

2 Stitch plastic canvas according to graphs, Overcasting wing edges with purple, pink or aqua according to graphs.

3 Whipstitch matching wings together along centers using black yarn.

4 *Antennae:* Using wire cutters, cut three 4-inch (10cm) pieces from chenille stem. Bend each into a V; curl ends toward outside. Referring to photo throughout, hot-glue base of antennae to reverse side of each butterfly.

5 Affix a piece of magnetic tape or hot-glue a button magnet to the reverse side of each butterfly over folded end of antennae.

COLOR KEY	
Yards	**Medium Weight Yarn**
2 (1.9m)	■ Aqua
2 (1.9m)	■ Pink
2 (1.9m)	■ Purple
1 (1m)	■ Lavender
1 (1m)	■ Rose
1 (1m)	■ Yellow
1 (1m)	⁄ Black Whipstitch

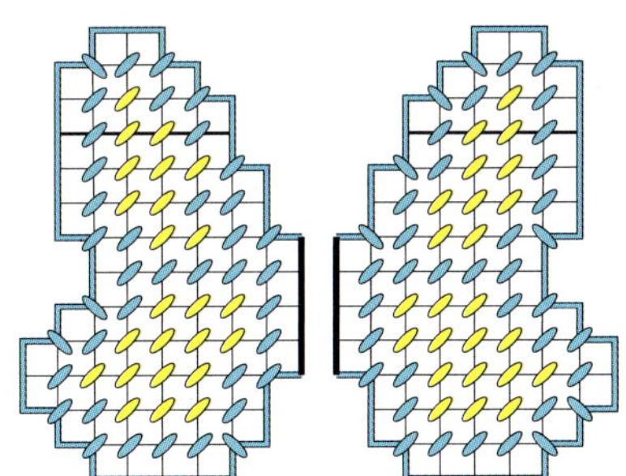

Aqua Butterfly Wings
8 holes x 13 holes
Cut 1 pair for each magnet
Cut 4 pairs for pastel tissue box

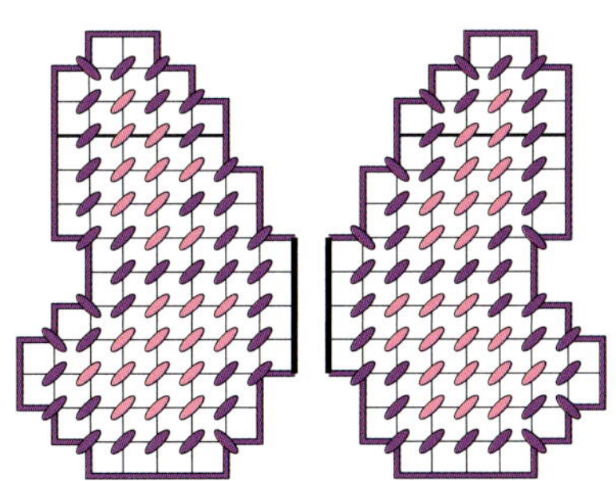

Purple Butterfly Wings
8 holes x 13 holes
Cut 1 pair for each magnet
Cut 1 pair for pastel tissue box

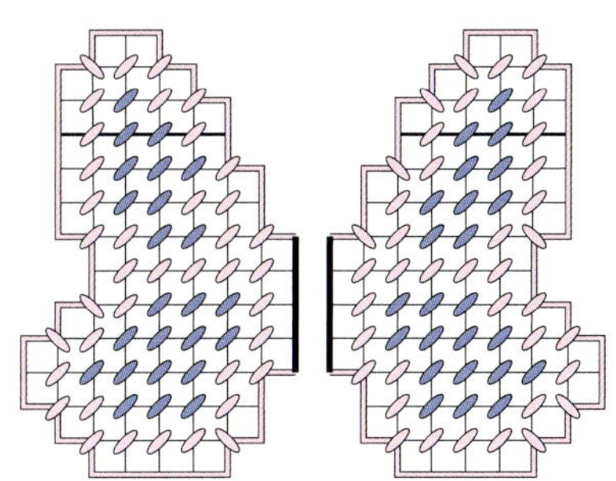

Pink Butterfly Wings
8 holes x 13 holes
Cut 1 pair for each magnet

Pastel Coasters

Size: **Coasters:** 4½ inches W x 4½ inches H (11.4cm x 11.4cm)
Holder: 4¾ inches W x 1⅝ inches H x 1½ inches D (12.1cm x 4.1cm x 3.8cm) excluding butterfly wings
Skill Level: Beginner

Materials

- ❑ 2 sheets clear 7-count plastic canvas
- ❑ Medium weight yarn as listed in color key
- ❑ #16 tapestry needle

Stitching Step by Step

1 Cut six coasters, coaster holder front and back, and two butterfly wings from plastic canvas according to graphs. Also cut two pieces 9 holes x 10 holes for coaster holder sides and one piece 31 holes x 9 holes for coaster holder bottom; bottom will remain unstitched.

2 Stitch coasters according to graph, filling in uncoded areas with light blue Continental Stitches. Overcast coasters with light blue.

3 Using black yarn, Straight Stitch butterfly antennae on coasters according to graph.

4 Stitch coaster holder front and back according to graphs, filling in uncoded areas with light blue Continental Stitches; fill in coaster holder sides with light blue Continental Stitches

5 Stitch butterfly wings according to graph, Overcasting aqua edges of wings as you stitch. Using black yarn throughout, Overcast remaining edges of butterflies where indicated outside arrows. Whipstitch butterflies between arrows to coaster holder front and back where indicated by red line on front/back graph.

6 Using light blue yarn throughout, Whipstitch coaster holder front, back and sides to one another along corners; Overcast top edges. Whipstitch assembled front, back and sides to bottom. Tuck coasters into holder.

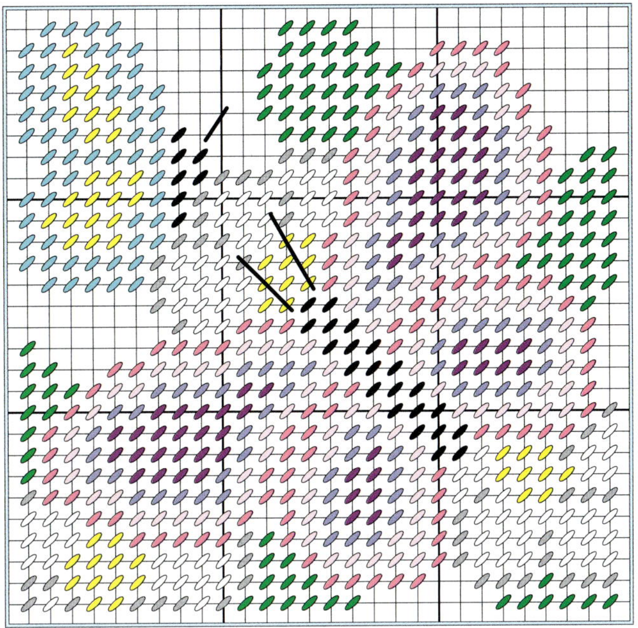

Pastel Coaster
29 holes x 29 holes
Cut 6

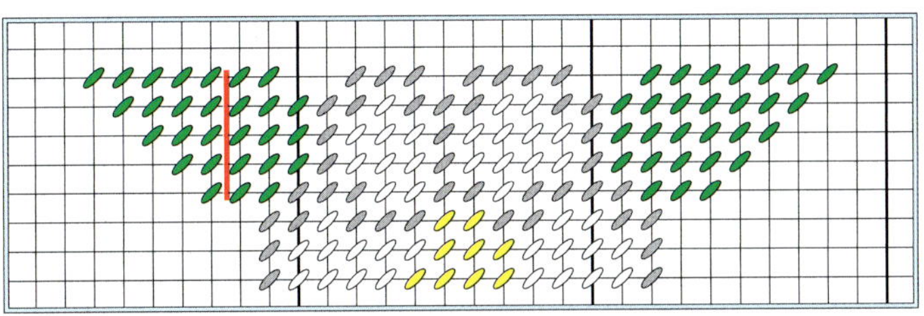

Pastel Coasters Holder Front/Back
31 holes x 10 holes
Cut 2

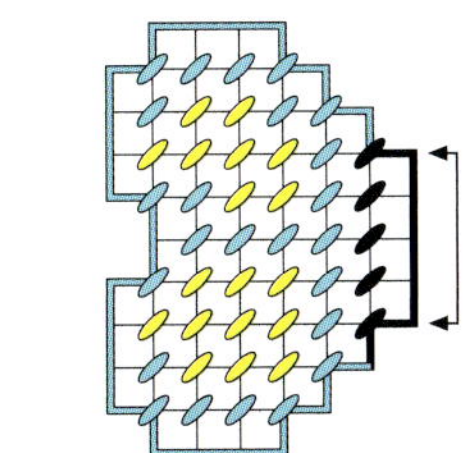

Pastel Coasters Butterfly Wings
7 holes x 10 holes
Cut 2

COLOR KEY

Yards	Medium Weight Yarn
9 (8.3m)	■ Green
9 (8.3m)	■ Rose
9 (8.3m)	■ Pink
8 (7.4m)	□ White
7 (6.5m)	■ Yellow
7 (6.5m)	■ Lavender
6 (5.5m)	■ Aqua
6 (5.5m)	■ Gray
6 (5.5m)	■ Purple
5 (4.6m)	■ Black
27 (24.7m)	Uncoded areas are light blue Continental Stitches
	⁄ Light blue Overcast and Whipstitch
	⁄ Black Straight Stitch

Pastel Tissue Box

Size: Fits boutique-style tissue box
Skill Level: Beginner

Materials

- ❑ 3 sheets clear 7-count plastic canvas
- ❑ Medium weight yarn as listed in color key
- ❑ #16 tapestry needle

Stitching Step by Step

Tissue Box

1 Cut top and four sides from plastic canvas according to graphs.

2 Stitch plastic canvas according to graphs, filling in uncoded areas with light blue Continental Stitches.

3 Using black yarn, Straight Stitch butterfly antennae on top and sides. Using light blue yarn, Overcast opening in top.

Butterflies

1 Cut one pair of purple butterfly wings and four pairs of aqua butterfly wings from plastic canvas according to graphs, page 13.

2 Stitch wings according to graphs, Overcasting purple and aqua edges as you stitch.

3 Referring to photo throughout and using black yarn through step 4, Whipstitch purple wings together along center for body; tack butterfly body to tissue box top where indicated by red line on graph.

4 Whipstitch body edge of aqua butterfly wings to tissue cover sides where indicated by red lines on graph, attaching a left-hand wing in upper left corner and a right-hand wing in lower right corner.

Assembly

Using light blue yarn throughout, Whipstitch tissue box sides to one another along corners; Overcast bottom edges. Whipstitch assembled sides to top.

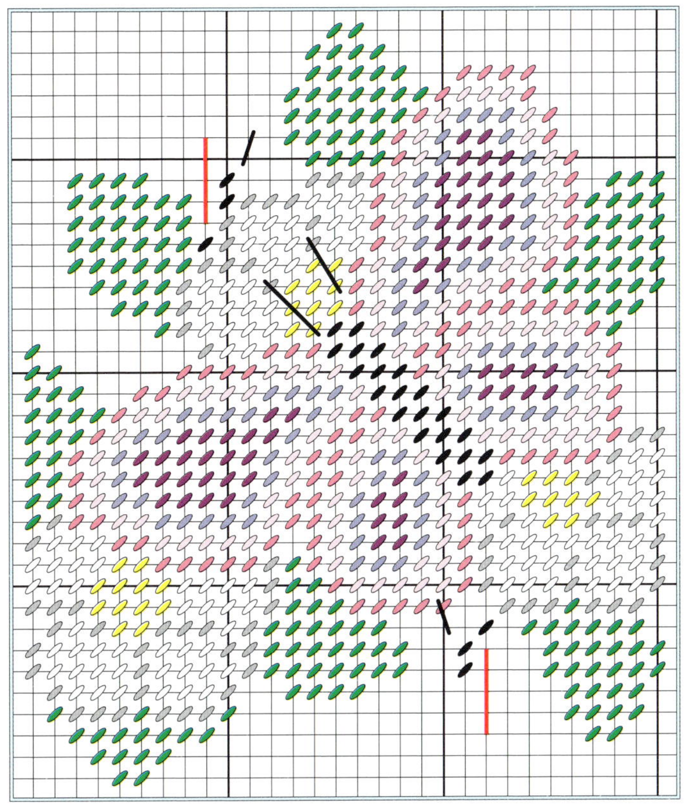

Pastel Tissue Box Side
31 holes x 37 holes
Cut 4

COLOR KEY	
Yards	**Medium Weight Yarn**
13 (11.9m)	Green
8 (7.4m)	Aqua
8 (7.4m)	Purple
8 (7.4m)	White
7 (6.5m)	Rose
6 (5.5m)	Pink
6 (5.5m)	Yellow
5 (4.6m)	Lavender
5 (4.6m)	Gray
3 (2.8m)	Black
30 (27.5m)	Uncoded areas are light blue Continental Stitches
	Light blue Overcast and Whipstitch
	Black Straight Stitch

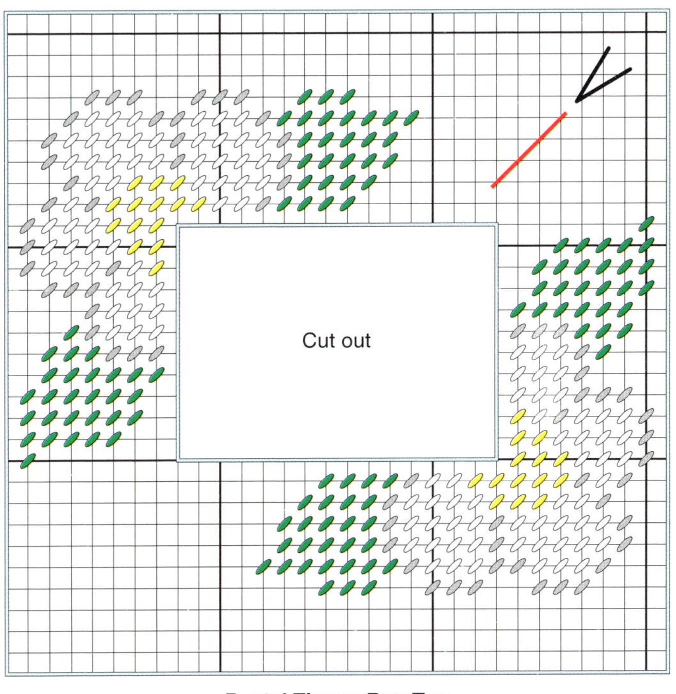

Pastel Tissue Box Top
31 holes x 31 holes
Cut 1

Butterfly Tissue Box
Instructions begin on page 1

Wall Hanging

Size: 12½ inches W x 12 inches H (31.75cm x 30.5cm), excluding hanger
Skill Level: Beginner

Materials

- ❑ 1 sheet clear 7-count plastic canvas
- ❑ Medium weight yarn as listed in color key
- ❑ 2 black chenille stems
- ❑ 4 inches (10.2cm) ¼-inch-wide (6mm) complementary satin ribbon
- ❑ #16 tapestry needle
- ❑ Wire cutters *or* craft nippers
- ❑ Hot-glue gun

Stitching Step by Step

1 Cut "Bath," two butterflies A and one each of butterflies B, C and D from plastic canvas according to graphs.

2 Stitch plastic canvas according to graphs, filling in uncoded areas with black Continental Stitches.

3 Overcast "Bath" with aqua. Overcast butterflies with adjacent colors according to graphs.

4 *Antennae:* Using wire cutters, cut five 4-inch (10. cm) pieces from chenille stems. Bend each into a V; curl ends toward outside. Referring to photo throughout, hot-glue base of antennae to reverse side of each butterfly.

5 Arrange butterflies and "Bath" in a circle as shown, overlapping edges slightly; hot-glue pieces together where they overlap.

6 Fold ribbon into a loop, crisscrossing ends. Hot-glue ribbon ends to reverse side of wall hanging at center top of "Bath."

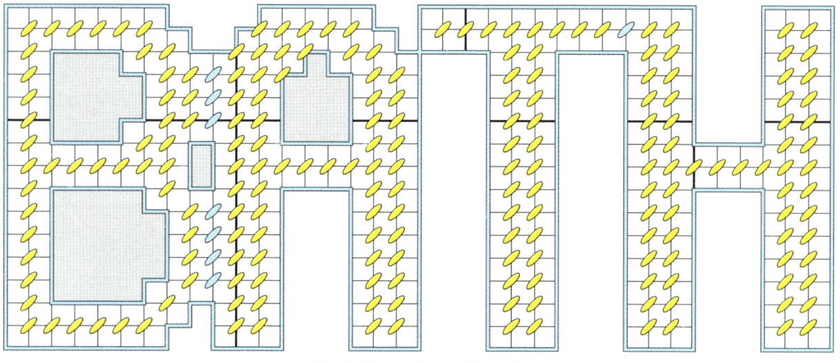

Wall Hanging "Bath"
36 holes x 15 holes
Cut 1, cutting away gray areas

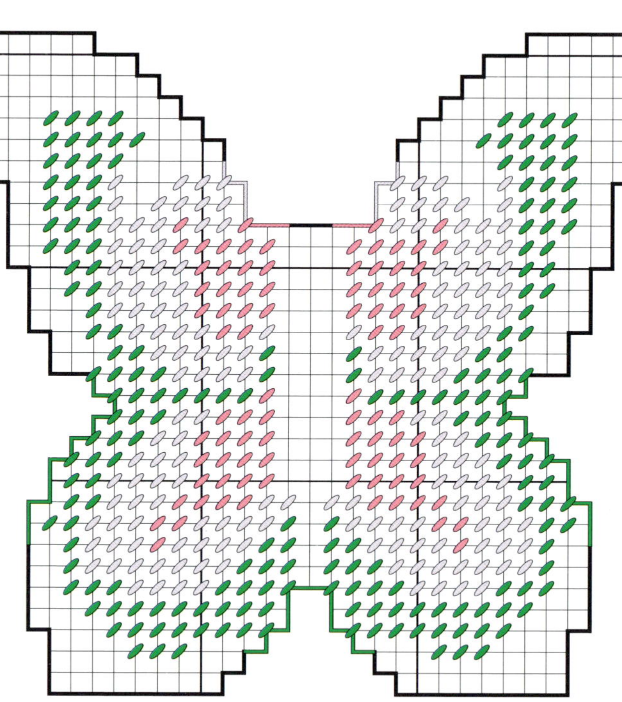

Butterfly B
30 holes x 31 holes
Cut 1 for wall hanging
Cut 1 for toilet paper caddy

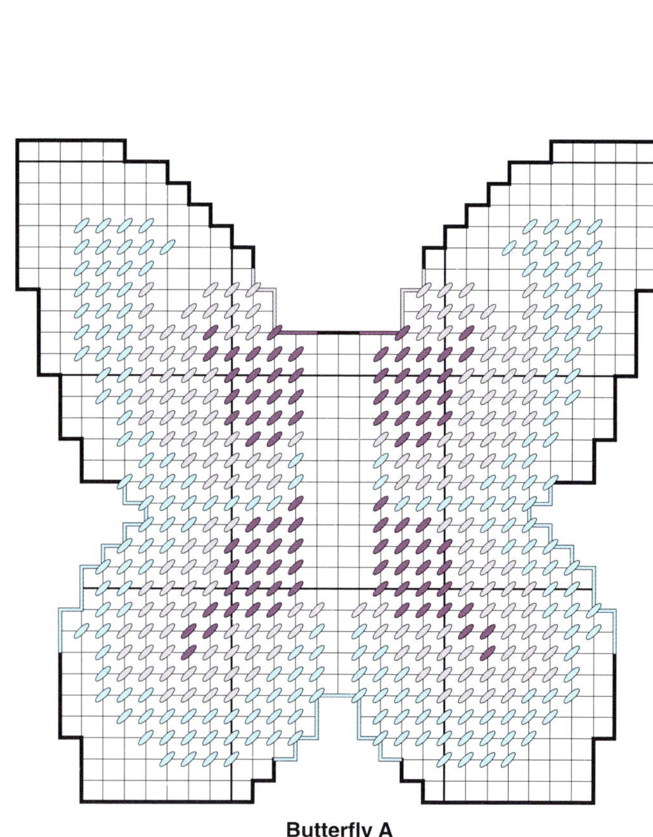

Butterfly A
30 holes x 31 holes
Cut 2 for wall hanging
Cut 2 for coasters

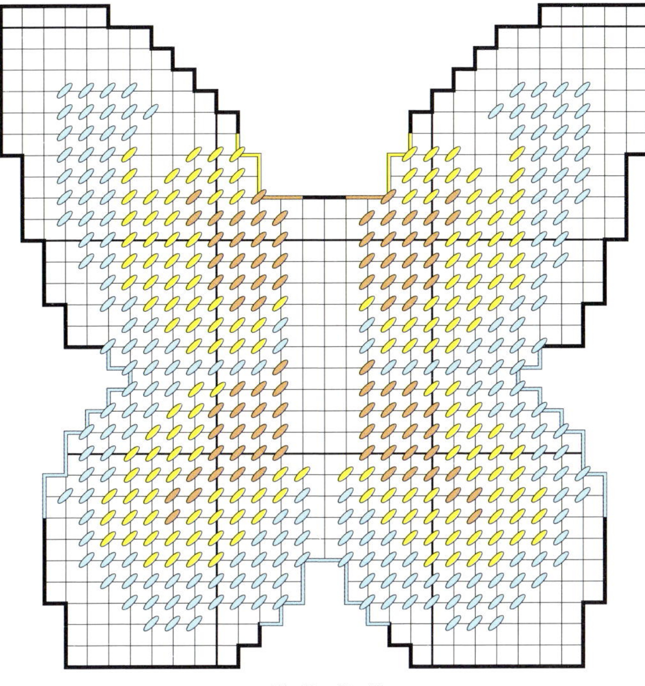

Butterfly C
30 holes x 31 holes
Cut 1 for wall hanging
Cut 1 for toilet paper caddy
Cut 2 for coasters

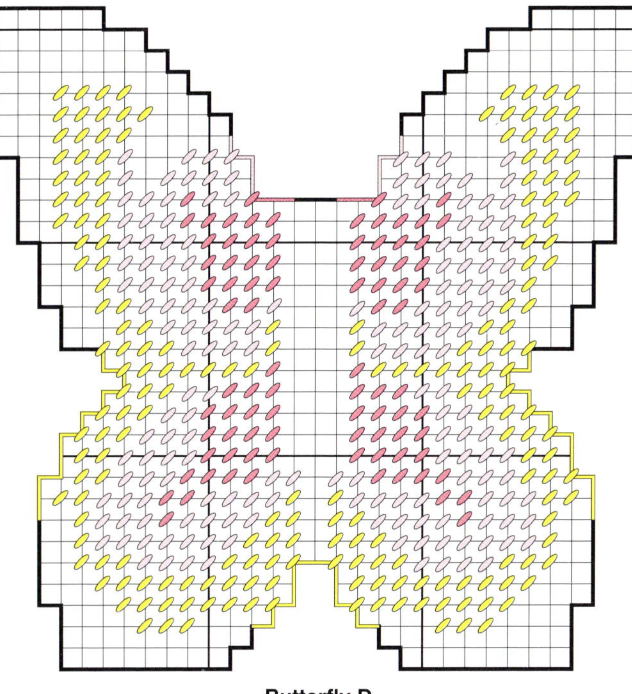

Butterfly D
30 holes x 31 holes
Cut 1 for wall hanging
Cut 1 for toilet paper caddy
Cut 2 for coasters

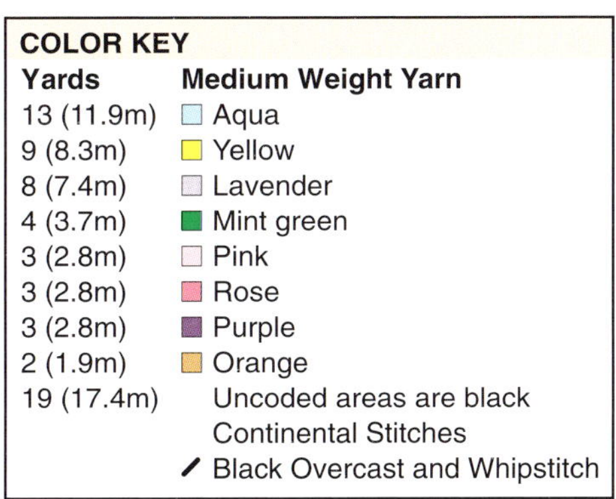

COLOR KEY

Yards	Medium Weight Yarn
13 (11.9m)	Aqua
9 (8.3m)	Yellow
8 (7.4m)	Lavender
4 (3.7m)	Mint green
3 (2.8m)	Pink
3 (2.8m)	Rose
3 (2.8m)	Purple
2 (1.9m)	Orange
19 (17.4m)	Uncoded areas are black Continental Stitches
	/ Black Overcast and Whipstitch

Toilet Paper Caddy

Size: 4½ inches W x 17½ inches H (11.4cm x 44.4cm); loops extend to hold 2 regular rolls of toilet paper
Skill Level: Beginner

Materials

- ❑ 3 sheets clear 7-count plastic canvas
- ❑ Medium weight yarn as listed in color key
- ❑ Black chenille stem
- ❑ 1-inch (2.5cm) plastic ring or other hanger
- ❑ #16 tapestry needle
- ❑ Wire cutters *or* craft nippers
- ❑ Hot-glue gun

Stitching Step by Step

1 Cut one toilet paper backing strip and one each of butterflies B, C and D, pages 20 and 21, according to graphs. Also cut two loop strips, each 7 holes x 80 holes.

2 Stitch butterflies according to graphs, filling in uncoded areas with black Continental Stitches. Overcast butterflies with adjacent colors according to graphs.

3 *Antennae:* Using wire cutters, cut three 4-inch (10cm) pieces from chenille stem. Bend each into a V; curl ends toward outside. Referring to photo throughout, hot-glue base of antennae to reverse side of each butterfly.

4 Fill loop strips and uncoded backing strip with white Continental Stitches, avoiding the yellow shaded area at the top of the backing strip.

5 Overcast long edges of loop strips and long edges of backing strip adjacent to white stitching with aqua.

Assembly & Finishing

1 Hold loop strips together, right sides facing, with bottom ends even. ***Optional:*** *For added stability, hot-glue the bottom 2 inches (5.1cm) of the strips together; let glue cool.* Using aqua yarn throughout, Whipstitch bottom ends of loop strips to right side of backing strip at red line B.

2 Whipstitch other end of top strip to backing strip at red line A. Whipstitch other end of bottom strip to bottom edge of backing strip at red line C; Overcast remainder of backing strip's bottom edge.

3 Stitch plastic ring or other hanger to reverse side of backing strip at center top.

4 Referring to photo throughout, hot-glue one butterfly to unstitched top of holder, over end of the top loop strip.

5 Hot-glue remaining butterflies to front of loops. Slide toilet paper rolls into loops.

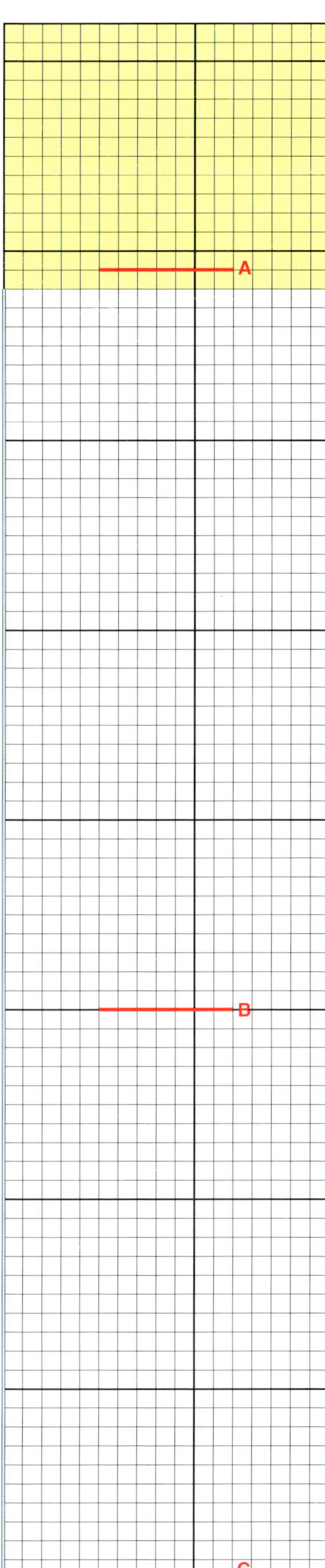

Toilet Paper Caddy Backing Strip
17 holes x 82 holes
Cut 1

COLOR KEY	
Yards	**Medium Weight Yarn**
10 (9.2m)	☐ Aqua
6 (5.5m)	■ Yellow
4 (3.7m)	■ Mint green
3 (2.8m)	☐ Lavender
3 (2.8m)	☐ Pink
3 (2.8m)	■ Rose
2 (1.9m)	■ Orange
33 (30.2m)	Uncoded area on backing strip is white Continental Stitches
12 (11m)	Uncoded areas on butterflies are black Continental Stitches
	⁄ Black Overcast and Whipstitch

The full line of The Needlecraft Shop products is carried by Annie's Attic catalog.
TOLL-FREE ORDER LINE
or to request a free catalog
(800) 582-6643
Customer Service
(800) 449-0440
Visit AnniesAttic.com

ISBN: 978-1-57367-325-9
Printed in USA
1 2 3 4 5 6 7 8 9

Shopping for Supplies

For supplies, first shop your local craft and needlework stores. Some supplies may be found in fabric, hardware and discount stores. If you are unable to find the supplies you need, please call Annie's Attic at (800) 582-6643 to request a free catalog that sells plastic canvas supplies.

Before You Cut

Buy one brand of canvas for each entire project as brands can differ slightly in the distance between bars. Count holes carefully from the graph before you cut, using the bolder lines that show each 10 holes. These 10-count lines begin in the lower left corner of each graph to make counting easier. Mark canvas before cutting; then remove all marks completely before stitching. If the piece is cut in a rectangular or square shape and is either not worked, or worked with only one color and one type of stitch, the graph is not included in the pattern. Instead, the cutting and stitching instructions are given in the general instructions or with the individual project instructions.

Covering the Canvas

Bring needle up from back of work, leaving a short length of yarn on back of canvas; work over short length to secure. To end a thread, weave needle and thread through the wrong side of your last few stitches; clip. Follow the numbers on the small graphs beside each stitch illustration; bring your needle up from the back of the work on odd numbers and down through the front of the work on even numbers. Work embroidery stitches last, after the canvas has been completely covered by the needlepoint stitches.

Basic Stitches

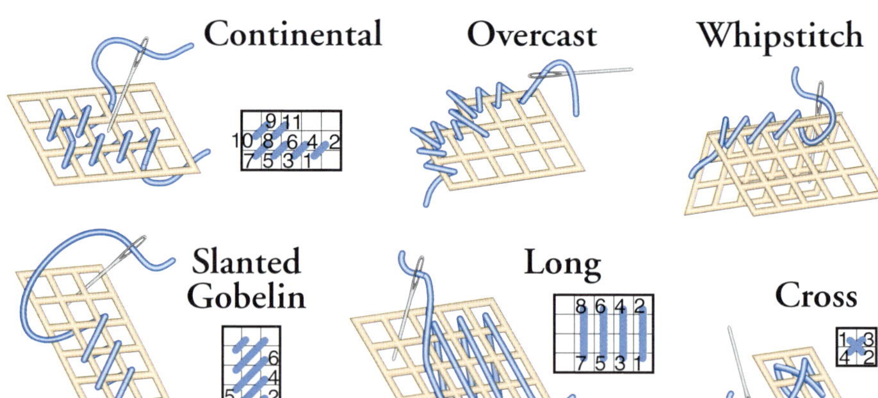

Embroidery Stitches

French Knot

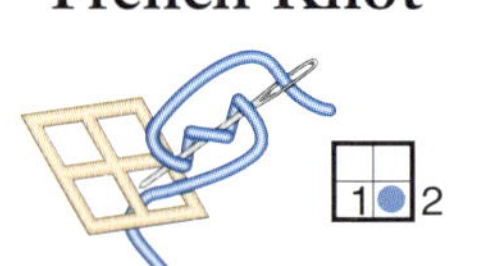

Lazy Daisy

Backstitch

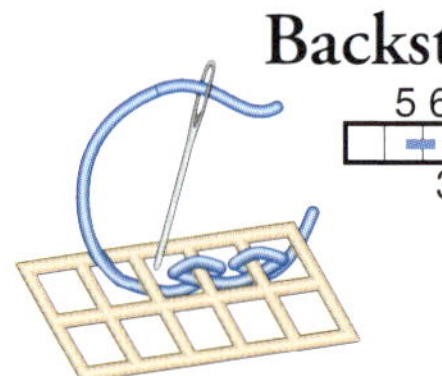

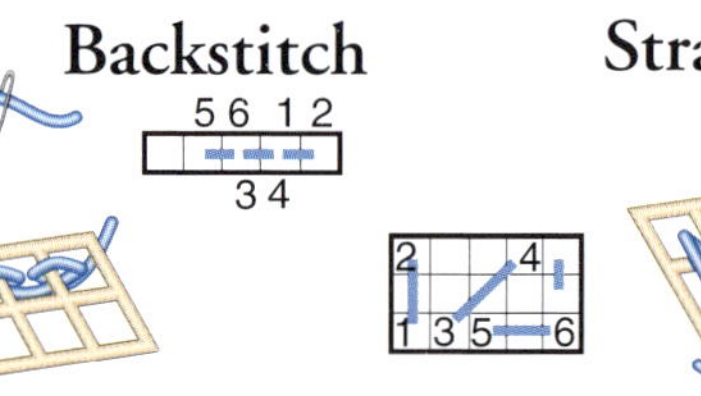

Straight

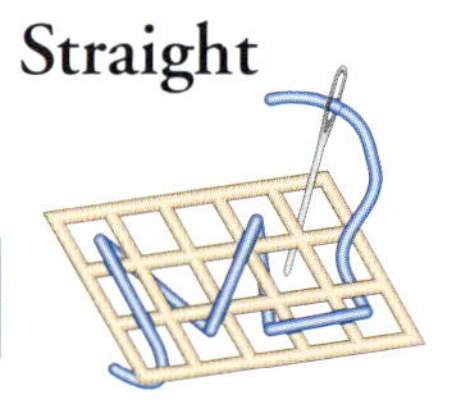

METRIC KEY:
millimeters = (mm)
centimeters = (cm)
meters = (m)
grams = (g)